# AUSTRIA

## WORLD ADVENTURES

### BY EMILIE DUFRESNE

BookLife

**BookLife**
PUBLISHING

©2018
**BookLife Publishing**
**King's Lynn**
**Norfolk PE30 4LS**

A catalogue record for this
book is available from the
British Library.

**ISBN:** 978-1-78637-511-7

**Written by:**
Emilie Dufresne

**Edited by:**
Robin Twiddy

**Designed by:**
Amy Li

# AUSTRIA
## WORLD ADVENTURES

## CONTENTS

Words that look like **this** can be found in the glossary on page 24.

# WHERE IS AUSTRIA?

Austria is a country in central Europe. It is completely surrounded by lots of different countries.

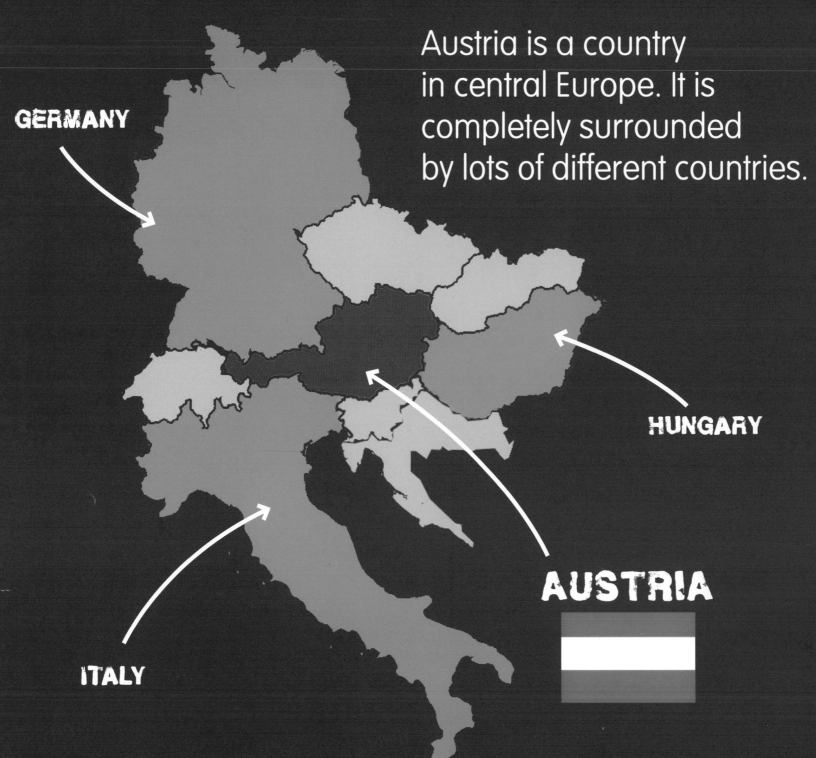

GERMANY

ITALY

HUNGARY

AUSTRIA

# VIENNA, AUSTRIA

The capital of Austria is Vienna.

Over eight million people live in Austria.
Most people in Austria live in towns and cities.

# WEATHER AND LANDSCAPE

LAKE WOLFGANG, AUSTRIA

The weather in Austria changes with the seasons. The coldest months are usually January and February and the warmest months are July and August.

Austria has lots of different types of landscapes. There are large lakes and towering mountains.

THE ALPS

MOUNTAIN RANGE

# CLOTHING

Most people in Austria wear modern clothing. Lots of people wear smart clothes for work and comfortable clothes at home.

LEDERHOSEN

DIRNDL

Lederhosen (say: lay-der-hosen) and dirndls (say: dern-duls) are **traditional** Austrian outfits. They used to be very popular but are now only worn on special occasions.

# RELIGION

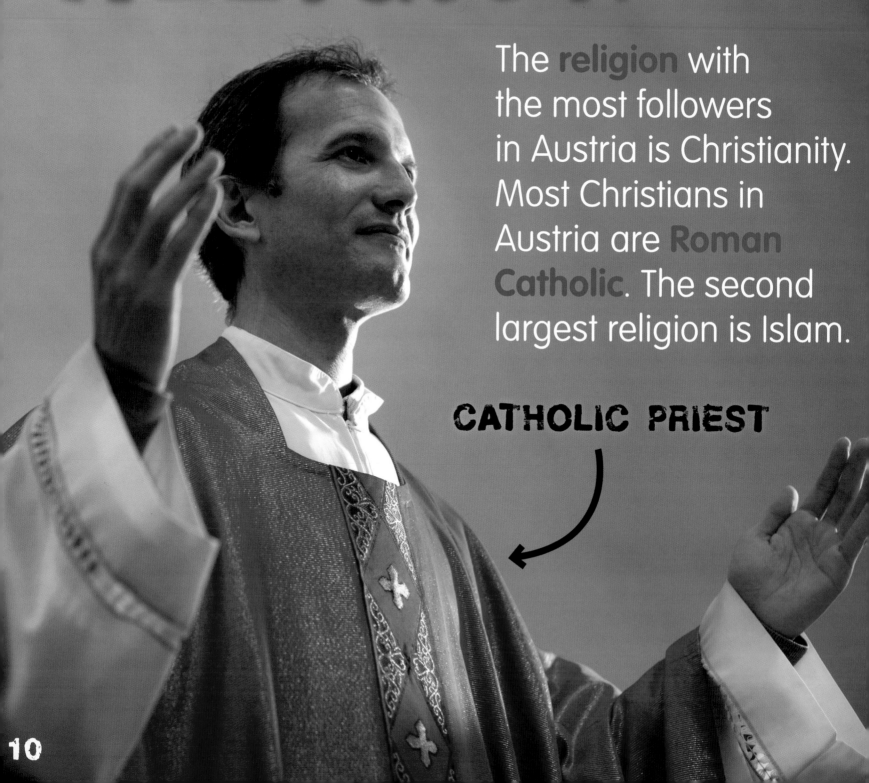

The **religion** with the most followers in Austria is Christianity. Most Christians in Austria are **Roman Catholic**. The second largest religion is Islam.

**CATHOLIC PRIEST**

# ST. STEPHEN'S CATHEDRAL, VIENNA

Roman Catholics worship in a church or cathedral. There are lots of cathedrals in Austria. Most Roman Catholics go to church every Sunday.

# FOOD

Wiener schnitzel is often served with potatoes and salad.

Wiener schnitzel is a traditional Austrian dish. It is made from a thin piece of meat which is coated in breadcrumbs and fried.

Austria is also known for its pastries. Strudel is a pastry that can be sweet or **savoury**. Apple strudel is made from stewed apples wrapped in puff pastry.

# AT SCHOOL

This girl is doing a **carpentry** apprenticeship.

In Austria, children have to stay in school until they are 15 years old. Students can then go on to do an apprenticeship.

On their first day of school, lots of Austrian children get a cone full of presents such as toys, chocolates and school supplies.

It's called a schultüte (say shool-toot-eh).

# AT HOME

Lots of people in Austria live in cities.
They usually live in apartments or flats.

APARTMENTS
IN VIENNA

Some people live in the countryside, in towns and villages. Lots of farmers live in the countryside where they grow lots of wheat, oats and rye.

# FAMILIES

Children in Austria usually live with their parents and **siblings**. Some children might have **godparents** or guardians.

Families in Austria come together to celebrate special **occasions** like birthdays or religious holidays such as Christmas and Easter.

# SPORT

Football, volleyball and ice hockey are all popular sports in Austria.

Winter sports are very popular in Austria. Many people go on skiing or snowboarding holidays.

# FUN FACTS

The Austrian flag is one of the oldest flags in the world. It was created in the 13th century.

The second longest river in Europe, the Danube, flows through Austria. The river passes nine different countries in total.

DANUBE RIVER, VIENNA

# GLOSSARY

| | |
|---|---|
| **apprenticeship** | a type of education where you learn through working |
| **carpentry** | working with and making things out of wood |
| **godparents** | adults that promise to take care of a child as well as their parents |
| **occasions** | special events to celebrate |
| **religion** | the belief in and worship of a god or gods |
| **Roman Catholic** | a type of Christianity |
| **savoury** | food that is salty or spicy, but not sweet |
| **siblings** | brothers and sisters |
| **traditional** | related to very old behaviours or beliefs |

# INDEX

**Photo Credits**
**All images are courtesy of Shutterstock.com, unless stated otherwise.**

Front Cover – The Hornbills Studio, Martina Zaletel, 1 – The Hornbills Studio, 2 – emperorcosar, 3 – Martina Zaletel, 4 – borelea, konstantinks, 5 – mRGB, 6 – leoks, 7 – canadastock, 8 – William Perugini, 9 – Kzenon, 10 – Diego Cervo, 11 – Shinda Lin, 12 – Tatiana Bralnina, 13 – YuliiaHolochenkov, 14 – Monkey Business Images, 15– TunedIn by westend61, 17 – Gaspar Janos, 18 – Alexey Fedorenko, 19 – S. Bonsov, 20 – Lucky Business, 21 – Dmitry Molchanov, 22 – casadphoto, 23 – mRGB, 24 – TheHornbills Studio